JERICHO

I0140115

Jack Canfora

BROADWAY PLAY PUBLISHING INC
New York
www.broadwayplaypublishing.com
info@broadwayplaypublishing.com

JERICHO
© Copyright 2012 by Jack Canfora

All rights reserved. This work is fully protected under the copyright laws of the United States of America. No part of this publication may be photocopied, reproduced, stored in a retrieval system, or transmitted, in any form or by any means, electronic, mechanical, recording, or otherwise, without the prior permission of the publisher. Additional copies of this play are available from the publisher.

Written permission is required for live performance of any sort. This includes readings, cuttings, scenes, and excerpts. For amateur and stock performances, please contact Broadway Play Publishing Inc. For all other rights contact the author c/o B P P I.

cover photo by Carol Rosegg

First printing: November 2012
This printing: October 2015
I S B N: 978-0-88145-556-4

Book design: Marie Donovan
Page make-up: Adobe Indesign
Typeface: Palatino
Printed and bound in the U S A

ABOUT THE AUTHOR

Jack Canfora's plays have been read and performed throughout the United States and England since 2001. The New Jersey Repertory Company staged his first full length play, PLACE SETTING, prompting *The New Jersey Star-Ledger* to name it, along with plays by Teresa Rebeck, Elaine May and Edward Albee, as one of the best plays of 2007.

His play POETIC LICENSE ran Off-Broadway at 59E59 Theaters in 2012. In November 2011, he won Abingdon Theatre's playwriting award for the play.

JERICHO was named a winner of the 2010 National New Play Network and premiered at The New Jersey Repertory Company, The Phoenix Theatre in Indianapolis, and the Florida Studio Theatre as part of the N N P N's Rolling World Premiere series.

His sketch comedy writing was frequently seen in Greenwich Village in the late 90s and on the main stage of the world famous comedy club Caroline's.

He is an English teacher at Plainview Old Bethpage John F Kennedy High School.

He has two children and lives in New York with his wife and dog.

The National New Play Network World Premiere of JERICHO was produced through the N N P N Continued Life Fund by the New Jersey Repertory Company (Long Branch, NJ,) Phoenix Theatre (Indianapolis, IN,) and Florida Studio Theatre (Sarasota, FL,) and was supported by a grant from the Edgerton Foundation New American Plays Award.

JERICHO received its world premiere on 15 October 2011, at the New Jersey Repertory Theatre in Long Branch, New Jersey (SuzAnne Barabas, Artistic Director, Gabor Barabas, Executive Director). The cast and creative contributors were as follows:

BETH..Corey Tazmania
DR KIM/ALEC..Matt Huffman
ETHAN..Andrew Rein
JESSICA.. Carol Todd
JOSH..Jim Shankman
RACHEL..Kathleen Goldpaugh

Director..Evan Bergman
Set designer... Jessica Parks
Lighting design.. Jill Nagle
Costume design...................................... Patricia E Doherty
Sound design...John Emmett O'Brien
Stage manager..Rose Riccardi

JERICHO premiered Off-Broadway at 59E59 Theatre on 10 October 2013. The cast and creatives were:

BETH...Eleanor Handley
DR KIM / ALEC..Kevin Isola
ETHAN ....Andrew Rein
JESSICA .... Carol Todd
JOSH .... Noel Allain
RACHEL.. Jill Eikenberry

Director...Evan Bergman
Set designer.. Jessica Parks
Lighting design .... Jill Nagle
Costume design...Michael McDonald
Sound design...John Emmett O'Brien
Stage manager...Rose Riccardi

CHARACTERS & SETTING

BETH
DR. KIM*
ALEC*
ETHAN
JESSICA
JOSH
RACHEL

*DR. KIM *and* ALEC a*re played by the same actor in the same costume*

Setting: A therapist's office, ETHAN's *Manhattan apartment,* JOSH *and* JESSICA's *Manhattan apartment,* RACHEL's *house on Jericho, Long Island*

Time: Circa 2005

The author wishes to thank Evan Bergman, SuzAnne Barabas, Gabor Barabas and the entire staff of the New Jersey Repertory Theatre for the their talents and support. He would also like to thank the National New Play Network for its invaluable assistance as well as the casts, crews and artistic staffs at the Phoenix Theatre and the Florida Studio Theatre.

For my parents, Jackie and Evan Bergman. And, as in pretty much all things, for Ben and Emma.

There's injustice everywhere/And no rebellion.
Bertolt Brecht

Oh, I have made myself a tribe/ Out of my true
affections/And my tribe is scattered!
Stanley Kunitz

I feel stupid and contagious/ Here we are now;
entertain us.
Kurt Cobain

ACT ONE

Scene One

(A therapist's office. A young man, about 30, sits on a comfortable chair with a notepad. He is the therapist. He is lit but not in the full light of the woman, about 35. She sits on couch or perhaps another comfortable chair. She is the patient. They are therapizing, engaging in muted conversation when we see the lights come up on them. After a moment or two of this, the woman addresses the audience directly.)

BETH: You know, there are times, if I'm honest about it, I think my husband being killed is the least of my problems. *(Pause)* Well. That came out wrong, didn't it? God, you know, most of my thoughts, as I'm thinking them, strike me as perfectly reasonable or at least, you know, well intentioned. But the minute I voice them... Well. Blame the pills. I am currently taking what medical experts call a shitload of medication. Not that my problems are solely chemically based, anyway. I have of course dabbled in the odd anti depressant before. I'm a well educated person living in Manhattan, so, you know, it's considered gauche not to. What I've found, though? It's that they, the pills I mean, make everything sort of...glazed. Which is not without its perks, I'm here to tell you. Your life coated in Lucite, like a museum exhibit. Visible but free from touch. *(Pause)* Although I have to say, before, before all of this, I was never someone who had her shit completely together, but there was a time when my shit was at least all within, you know, walking distance.

DR KIM: (*"Are you paying attention to me?"*) Beth?

BETH: (*To* DR KIM) Sorry! I did zone out there for a sec.

DR KIM: I thought so. (*He now once again mimes the give and take of conversation*)

BETH: (*Back now to us*) I feel bad. About what I said before, about Alec's death being the least of it. It's not that I'm not overwhelmed by it. I am. I am, in fact, utterly…capsized. Hence the meds. But. The struggle to, I don't know, to get through it, somehow, it eludes me. The point of it. I don't know if that's survivor's guilt or whatever, or any of my other endless nuanced varieties of—you know the Eskimos? How they have umpteen words for snow? This is me with guilt. I'm the Ben & Jerry's of guilt. And when it comes to Alec, I…and it's a little monstrous to think that therapy's going to be able to smooth that over. You know? There are some things it should be impossible to recover from.

DR KIM: Beth?

BETH: Yeah, I'm here. Promise.

DR KIM: So. I've been wondering. It's…I look the same to you?

BETH: Yeah…the same, pretty much. Still, it's nothing to worry about. That's what you said.

DR KIM: My point is that while in and of itself it's nothing to, to, let's say panic about, I think we need to explore why in eight months it hasn't changed at all.

BETH: Ah, that's the part we should panic about. (*Pause*) I see your point about it. I mean being concerned about it.

DR KIM: Mm-hmn.

BETH: I can. *(Pause)* But it's not terrible, you know, it's not watchmacallit, transference—

DR KIM: Actually, it *is* a sort of trans—

BETH: Yes, but you know, it's not like I'm in love or want to have sex with you, or whatever. That's not what's happening here.

DR KIM: True.

BETH: No offense.

DR KIM: I'll recover.

BETH: And it's not like I'm confusing you for him.

DR KIM: No.

BETH: You know, thinking you *are* him or something. That would be...well, creepy.

DR KIM: That's the clinical term for it, yes.

BETH: It was an observation I made, that's all. And it's not just me. If other people knew the two of you, they'd say the same thing, I'll bet.

DR KIM: About Alec and me looking alike.

BETH: Absolutely. In a way.

DR KIM: Yes?

BETH: Yeah, not as much as I think you two do, probably, I mean, there's clearly a psychological component at work here.

DR KIM: Probably.

BETH: But it's not *entirely*, you know, made up. I've shown you his picture.

DR KIM: Yes, you have.

BETH: And...and you don't see the resemblance at all, do you?

DR KIM: Well, the picture you showed me, Alec was about thirty, light brown hair, green eyes.

BETH: Yes.

DR KIM: Whereas, I, of course, am a forty-seven year old Korean-American woman.

BETH: Well, you're dwelling on the obvious things, the superficial.

DR KIM: Yes, but I mean, as you see me here, right now, you see a thirtyish white man, right? It's not that Alec sat the same way as I do or laughed at the same things…

BETH: It's not like I think he's still alive or come back from the dead. And you do by the way. Laugh at a lot of the same sorts of things.

DR KIM: But it's not like that for you. You, you hear his voice, you, looking at my chair, see Alec.

BETH: Yeah.

DR KIM: Well it's not, in other aspects, affecting your ability to judge reality. But what I think we have to start questioning a little more deeply is what you're deriving from this. Especially now that you're starting to reengage in different aspects of your life…

BETH: "Reengage"?

DR KIM: By reengage I meant with you dating again.

BETH: I don't like that term.

DR KIM: Why?

BETH: I don't know…I…you're right, though. I'm… well, whatever I am doing with Ethan, whatever you call it…

DR KIM: I think it's a positive thing, by the way.

BETH: You do?

DR KIM: Absolutely.

BETH: Yeah. I do too, I guess. No: I *do*. I mean, I don't know what will happen, of course, but—

DR KIM: It shows faith.

BETH: Faith?

DR KIM: In you, in your life; that you won't, won't always...how do I put it?

BETH: Be as fucked up as a Japanese game show?

DR KIM: That you believe there are things to look forward to.

BETH: Yeah. I do believe that. I do. What I'm working on now is not feeling guilty about it.

DR KIM: It's ok to look forward to things.

BETH: I know. I mean, I want that. I do. I am looking forward. Or at least, you know, trying to.

DR KIM: These things take time.

BETH: Sure. Rome wasn't made not crazy in a day.

DR KIM: Have you told him about our sessions?

BETH: That I see you? Or that I see you as Alec?

DR KIM: Well...both.

BETH: No. Well, he knows I see a therapist, a nice woman who was recommended to me by the 9/11 grief posse...and obviously he knows about Alec, but the whole morphing of you and Alec I have going—I'm not sure how you slip that one in a conversation. Being psychotic.

DR KIM: You're not psychotic.

BETH: Doctor Kim, I think there's a book in this for you if you play your cards right. Maybe get a syndrome named after you. Hardly seems fair to me by the way that the syndrome would be named after you—I mean I'm the one who has it.

DR KIM: Yes, but I'd be the one who discovered it.

BETH: Because I told you.

DR KIM: Touche. You're clever.

BETH: Thanks.

DR KIM: Very clever. And articulate—I think we need to try making you less so.

BETH: Yeah.

DR KIM: Oh—I think I saw your ad on T V last week.

BETH: My ad?

DR KIM: Yes, the one with the cereal.

BETH: Oh, well, you know, it's not *my* ad—I just decorate the sets. I just know what looks best on camera.

DR KIM: Like the cereal—the—what was it you use instead of milk?

BETH: Glue.

DR KIM: Glue. Right. *(Pause)* How go the meds?

BETH: Fine. I guess. I'm toying with just hiring a game warden to drive by twice a day in a Range Rover and fire tranquilizers at me. I don't know if the insurance will cover that, though.

DR KIM: I hate to break it to you, but you're not psychotic. Something happened to you—

BETH: To Alec.

DR KIM: And therefore to *you*— something happened which is beyond comprehension. Unprecedented.

BETH: No. I can't deal with it if it's…I mean he died. These things…they happen. That this happened as part of a famous, historic thing, I can't help, but if I try to process it in those terms…I can't. If I conceive of it as part of this thing that will one day bore kids in Social Studies, you know…it stops meaning anything. It's grief. And it's unbearable, but the one thing it is not is unprecedented. Dying young, dying violently, without reason or fairness or pity or…it's not unprecedented.

DR KIM: Alec dying is unprecedented.

(Pause)

BETH: Yes.

(Blackout)

Scene Two

(BETH and ETHAN in a living room-ish environment. They are sitting/reclining casually with each other watching T V and scavenging through the remains of their take out Chinese dinner.)

BETH: This is the thing. I mean, forget the museums or Shakespeare in the Park or whatever—the main reason I could never go back to Michigan—the reason I couldn't ever really leave Manhattan is the Chinese food.

ETHAN: They don't have Chinese food in Michigan?

BETH: Well, they think they do.

ETHAN: There's a place near my mom's house in Jericho—we ate there every week practically, if you want—we'll go there sometime—the lo mein is unreasonably good.

BETH: Excellent. Speaking of which—how long were you debating?

ETHAN: Debating?

BETH: I mean Thanksgiving at your mother's. You said you were debating it.

ETHAN: Oh—not— you know, debate's a strong word, you know, it's not like I'd set up podiums. But it's, my family, they're, they can be a little…it's tough for me to describe. I'd had hoped to work up a power point thing for you on them.

BETH: Alec used to say that every family's crazy. Even the well adjusted ones.

BETH: Yeah.

BETH: Sorry, was that…?

ETHAN: No it's fine. What, I mean are you not supposed to talk about him? You guys were married, I get it.

BETH: Yeah but I do it without thinking sometimes. You're not in—I mean, I don't want you to, to think you're in competition with a, a—

ETHAN: With someone who's been dead four years.

BETH: Right.

ETHAN: I didn't mean, that sounded—

BETH: No, you're right. And you're, you're not. I mean it's not that I'm comparing you or, or am thinking about him or…oh, God, Beth *please* stop talking. Ironically another thing Alec would sometimes say. (*Beat. She smiles sheepishly*)

ETHAN: It's O K.

BETH: Your family. Tell me about—you were talking about your family. Reassuring me, I believe, that they're not crazy.

ETHAN: I mean, they're like medium-size crazy.

BETH: That doesn't sound too bad.

ETHAN: And the Thanksgiving thing. I didn't want to scare you off or anything, make you think it was this thing.

BETH: Well, it is something, right?

ETHAN: It's…few times a year my mother feels that we need to do these things…she guilts me and then I do it to my brother and his wife, or vice versa—my whole family's a sort of an emotional pyramid scheme, basically.

BETH: My kind of people.

ETHAN: Put it this way—I didn't anguish over it as long as you have about answering me. Which you still haven't.

BETH: Yeah. Well. I don't know.

ETHAN: Well then, O K, I think we have our answer, no?

BETH: No, it's not—

ETHAN: Forget about it.

BETH: Don't be like that. I…I really want to. And it's not like I, I hadn't started thinking about holiday stuff. It's I sort of had plans.

ETHAN: Ah. With?

(BETH *is not sure how to answer, which in itself answers the question*)

ETHAN: Ah. Alec's family.

BETH: Yeah.

ETHAN: O K then.

BETH: Well, I'm sorry, I don't know what that—I can't erase them from my life. I mean, I don't want to even if I could.

ETHAN: Let me ask you—honestly—have I given the impression *at all* that I wanted or, or ex*pec*ted you to, to *erase* him from your memory? That I would ever in any way expect—

BETH: *(Conceding)* No; no you haven't. You've been so—

ETHAN: O K then, but that's still your answer every time this comes up, which is more often than I would've guessed when we started—dating, is it, is it O K to—are we officially dating?

BETH: Are we—yes. of course.

ETHAN: I mean, I've been, I think, I *hope* I've been, certainly understanding, and patient with everything, but I, you know about three months in, I want a, a rel*a*tionship. You know? And that means, you know—

BETH: *(over "that means, you know –")* I know, you're right. You're—

ETHAN: *(over "you're right. You're")* I mean even this whole sex thing…

BETH: Or lack thereof. I know, you've been so—so understanding…

ETHAN: And I mean, not to bring it up again, you know, I don't want to…I don't know…

BETH: Beat off a dead horse?

(ETHAN laughs at this. It lowers the temperature.)

ETHAN: In a manner of…that's the thing…you have no problem *joking* with me about it—

BETH: It's the shittiest of defense mechanisms, I know. It's not like I'm not…I mean I do like sex…if memory serves, even if I've only slept with three men in my life—although considering my Muslim-Irish Catholic lineage, I'm sort of an uber-slut. I swear to you, Ethan, I swear, in my mind, we've had loads of Olympic-

level, Cinemax-at-two-in-the-morning kind of sex. I
know that doesn't do you much good. It's the intimacy
thing...

ETHAN: I know.

BETH: Give me a little time.

ETHAN: I'm trying.

BETH: I know. I'm sorry.

ETHAN: I'm, I'm sorry too. It's just, I don't know.

BETH: I know. Just a little more time. I'm sorry. *(She
moves toward him, or on him suggestively.)* Let me make
you cum.

ETHAN: No, Beth, it's—it feels like you feel you owe to
me.

BETH: Well, I sort of do.

ETHAN: Jesus. No! It's not community service.

BETH: It's a good thing, Ethan. It's intimacy, it's as close
as I can get at this moment. I know it's not much...is it
that I'm bad at it?

ETHAN: Oh my God, no.

BETH: I probably am. I'm a bit rusty...

ETHAN: God no. Quite the—last time was
unbelievable—I wrote my councilman, actually, the
next morning to see if I could get a park or something
named after you. So. No, it's...I need more.

BETH: I know.

ETHAN: I'm not trying to give an ultimatum or
anything or—I'm sorry.

BETH: Talking to me about this is probably like
planning a parade through a mine field. There's
nothing about it that doesn't suck, basically. For both

of us. I know. Please believe me, I know. You've been so…it's amazing, what you've been.

ETHAN: If you wait until you're ready, you'll never be ready.

BETH: Yeah. When you think about it, it's really the only thing we ever fight about really.

ETHAN: Yeah. But it's, it's there.

BETH: Yeah.

(Pause)

ETHAN: Look…it's silly to stress ourselves over this and…it'll be easier if you don't come this year.

BETH: Yeah.

ETHAN: A little patience. Next year in Jerusalem. Or Nassau County, anyway.

BETH: Hmm?

ETHAN: Next year in—it's an expression—a Jewish expression.

BETH: Oh. What's it mean?

ETHAN: Well, it means, at Passover, that we resolve to be in Jerusalem to celebrate the holiday next year.

BETH: That's a nice sentiment.

ETHAN: Yes, quite poignant, in a Zionist sort of way.

BETH: Well, there is that.

ETHAN: Anyway. And I mean it's…it's—we can see each other later. If you want.

BETH: Yeah…absolutely…trade war stories…enjoy working off the tryptophan together…

ETHAN: Yeah. *(They embrace, kissing each other with a mid level intensity that, for them, is a step forward. Then a pause)* It's better this way then. For now.

BETH: Yeah. For now.

(BETH *and* ETHAN *find a position on the couch for themselves and watch T V, comfortable, for the moment, with each other. Pause)*

BETH: Thank you. For saying all the things you've just said. About being patient.

ETHAN: Yeah, I, of—not a problem.

BETH: I do want to go with you.

ETHAN: It's O K, honestly.

BETH: No, I mean, this year. Let's do it.

ETHAN: I said it's fine. You've got Alec's family.

BETH: I don't know. I'll…think of something. I mean, I can't go back there every year, it's…it's a little like… I'm the proof he existed. It's compelling but so, so unhealthy.

ETHAN: No. I mean, I don't know.

BETH: No. It is. All that…goddamned…sympathy.

ETHAN: Yeah…it's…yeah.

BETH: It's awful. *(Pause)* Fucking awful. *(Pause. Then, a quiet and profound realization)* Can I say something to you?

ETHAN: Course.

BETH: I really…Alec would've liked you. *(Pause)* God… I'm sorry. That must be…be so weird to hear.

ETHAN: No. A little. *(Pause)* I…it's good though, right?

BETH: Yes. *(She holds his hand in both of hers—indicates his hand.)* This…this is the right thing…the healthy thing. Now.

(BETH *and* ETHAN *kiss.)*

(Lights fade.)

Scene Three

(A different but not dissimilar living room. Perhaps the couch and chair used in ETHAN'*s apartment are simply rearranged. This is the home of* ETHAN'*s older brother* JOSH *and his wife* JESSICA. JOSH *is watching a downstage T V and* JESSICA *enters.)*

JESSICA: Turn it off. Please.

JOSH: I'm watching it.

JESSICA: I pieced that together, actually. I don't want to watch it. Certainly not for the third time tonight.

JOSH: So therefore, it goes off.

JESSICA: It is, I repeat, the third news story on this thing tonight. The first two were lying?

JOSH: If they show that bloody, bandaged head one more…completely slanted coverage. Each time. You'd think he was the victim, they way they—

JESSICA: Then turn it off.

JOSH: Fine. *(With an unconcealed contempt) Access Hollywood* it is.

JESSICA: You have this charming way of saying the names of my shows that implies that watching them is the moral equivalent of sodomizing kittens.

JOSH: If you had any idea how hard it was to get that voice down.

JESSICA: Your mother watches this show, you know. *(Beat)* Wow. That was a dumb argument.

JOSH: I'm glad it was you who said it.

JESSICA: The point being, it would be nice if you could find it in your morally indignant heart to not equate my passing interest in movies and who's doing who in Hollywood—

JOSH: Who's doing whom.

JESSICA: Grammar? Are you kidding me? Anyway. If you could not equate who's doing WHOM in Hollywood with strapping dynamite to my chest and blowing up a bus load of school kids.

JOSH: I thought we'd agreed that these kind of exaggerations get us nowhere.

JESSICA: No, you and Doctor Liebman agreed to that, I thought we'd agreed that starting of sentences with "I thought we'd agreed that" was incredibly smug and irritating.

JOSH: Why are you so cranky?

JESSICA: I don't remember, to be honest, but the grammar lesson couldn't have helped.

JOSH: Trying to be helpful.

JESSICA: Josh, no one, anywhere, at any time, has ever corrected someone else's grammar in order to be helpful.

JOSH: O K.

JESSICA: "O K"?

JOSH: O K is somehow disagreeable now?

JESSICA: It's the context of the O K.

JOSH: What context? What are you—can we please not do this, I'm exhausted.

JESSICA: You're right. Sorry. We're both tired. *(Pause)* Can I have the remote, please?

JOSH: *(Indicating* Access Hollywood) I turned it on for you.

JESSICA: Yeah, I know, can I have it though?

JOSH: You need it louder? I'll make it louder.

JESSICA: Oh my God, I am not symbolically castrating you, I just want to be able to flip—I have to go through this ridiculous Freudian rigmarole with you and the remote twice a week.

JOSH: Don't give me your mishegas psychobabble— sometimes a remote is just a remote. I'm not thinking of castration.

JESSICA: That makes one of us. Please.

(JOSH *hands it to* JESSICA.)

JESSICA: Thank you. I'll be gentle.

JOSH: Thank you, as it's a stand in for my penis.

JESSICA: Which is odd 'cos if I remember, there aren't nearly as many buttons.

JOSH: *(Pause)* Rigmarole?

JESSICA: Well, you know, I'm tired.

(*Pause.* JESSICA *watches T V.* JOSH *picks up a book. A few seconds of silence. Then the phone rings.*)

JESSICA: I will pay you fifty dollars to answer that. Fifty dollars, American, hard currency.

JOSH: Machine'll get it.

JESSICA: *(Picks up handset, which is nearby, and reads the caller I D)* Your mother.

JOSH: Hm.

JESSICA: What about "Honor thy father and mother"?

JOSH: Yes, well, we can let the machine honor her tonight.

JESSICA: But she leaves these epic, Russian-novel-length messages. She *filibusters* into the machine.

JOSH: Ah, but I turned the sound down earlier tonight. (*The machine picks up the call*)

JESSICA: You see, then you go and do something like that and make me fall in love with you again. *(Pause)* You know what she's calling about, of course.

JOSH: Yeah.

JESSICA: All the more reason not to pick up, I suppose.

(JOSH gives a perfunctory nod)

JESSICA: So…what are we going to say to her?

JOSH: What do you want to say?

JESSICA: Ethan be there?

JOSH: Think so, yeah. In fact, I know he is. He's bringing a date.

JESSICA: *(Intrigued)* Really? How intriguing.

JOSH: Mm-hmm. She's not Jewish.

JESSICA: You *asked* him if she was Jewish?

JOSH: I'm not sure why that would be such an outrageous question and no, he volunteered that she wasn't Jewish.

JESSICA: Well, according to you, neither are the rest of us.

JOSH: I've never said anything like that at all. I point out, sometimes, certainly, that we—you—don't observe—

JESSICA: Please, let's not…*(She waves her hand. Considers)* So, Ethan's going. I gotta say, I think we have to go.

JOSH: Yeah?

JESSICA: *(Noticing machine)* Is she still going? *(She confirms that the machine's still recording)* What the hell? What could she possibly have left to say?

(JESSICA turns up the volume, revealing RACHEL's voice)

RACHEL: to order—they said we had to call the order in by this week, but I remember they said that last

year and we didn't they still got it done in time,
obviously, so don't worry, on the other hand, we didn't
get the stuffing we asked for—I think—or was it the
cranberry—I can't remember—there was something
that wasn't as we ordered, I remember—no, wait,
it—I know what it was—the stuffing had cranberry,
in it—and it's always given Ethan horrible gas so we
have to not—hang on—I'm just writing myself a note
here— "no…cranberry in stuff….Ethan…gas" —sorry,
anyway—and so you know I don't think we should,
you know *shoot* for being late with the order, so I'm
thinking, let's see, tomorrow I'll be home at about—

(JESSICA *turns sound off.*)

JESSICA: This is the reason we've gone through three
machines in two years—they've committed suicide.
(Pause) I don't really mind. Going. I mean, she, she
has her *quirks*, obviously, but I like your mother. And
Ethan.

JOSH: Yeah.

JESSICA: We share the same pagan aesthetic.

JOSH: I don't think you're pagans.

JESSICA: Whatever.

JOSH: It's just this…I mean, filling your mind with this
shit. *(Indicates T V)*

JESSICA: I'm not filling my mind with it. I'm
watching it. It's entertain—know how exhausting it
is to justify myself all the time? This constant air of
disappointment. It's just a television show.

JOSH: So smart, so educated, how can you be
entertained by this crap is all.

JESSICA: *(This speech should build to a crescendo of
sorts)* Because, Josh, they've gotten to me, O K? It's
time I come clean—they got to me. I'm—you know,

wandering the desert, worshipping golden goddamned calves, I'm—I'm—one of the lost, the great unwashed, the damned. Now can I watch my fucking show in peace for two minutes so—I can have something to chat about around the water cooler when I end up in the 9th Circle of Hell?

JOSH: *(Pause)* Hell has water coolers?

JESSICA: Yes, but they're always empty. Irony's huge there.

JOSH: Sorry.

JESSICA: I'm serious, Josh, I will not spend my life feeling like I forgot my homework and the teacher's walking down my row to check.

JOSH: I don't try to make you feel that way.

JESSICA: I know, but you do. *(Pause)* Have you made up your mind yet?

JOSH: About...no. I don't know. I want you to come with me.

JESSICA: I can't.

JOSH: Why?

JESSICA: Please not again.

JOSH: Why?

JESSICA: They're crazy there.

JOSH: You keep—who?

JESSICA: Everyone.

JOSH: Everyone in Israel's crazy? You're saying this?

JESSICA: Well, I haven't met everyone, but it seems to be their unleavened bread and butter, yes.

JOSH: You're deliberately antagonizing me.

JESSICA: No, I'm being honest. If I were deliberately antagonizing you, I'd point out this praying five hundred times a day and having separate plates for dairy and this "we belong in Israel" mantra comes from a man who ate lobster at our non-denominational wedding.

JOSH: None of that's relevant to now. Or why you won't go with me.

JESSICA: Place scares me.

JOSH: Well, I can understand that. It kind of scares me too. But this place should scare you just as much. More, actually, because everyone's got their heads up their asses.

JESSICA: Please, with the lectures. No, it's not the—the people scare me Josh, not just the place or situation, the actual people.

JOSH: The Arabs? Of course they do, they should. That's part of the point of going, to stand up to them.

JESSICA: Everyone there scares me. Yes, the Arabs. Yes. Of course the Arabs. The Jews too. More so.

JOSH: More so?

JESSICA: Ten times more.

JOSH: How can your own people scare you?

JESSICA: Because they're my own people.

(Pause)

JOSH: Please. Think about it. A little.

JESSICA: I know. I am. You think there's no *Access Hollywood* in Israel?

JOSH: Of course there is. That's not really the point.

JESSICA: No? *(Pause)* So are we going to your mother's? Thanksgiving?

JOSH: I think you're right.

JESSICA: About?

JOSH: Ethan. If he's going, we probably should too.

JESSICA: Yeah. Well, the girlfriend will make it interesting, maybe.

JOSH: Yeah. I'm sorry, Jess, I'm...I really do want us to...I just don't think I can stay here. I think I need to go.

JESSICA: Yeah. Well, then, I guess it's a good thing we're probably getting divorced.

JOSH: *(Pause)* Yeah.

(Blackout)

Scene Four

(DR KIM's office)

BETH: His brother's crazy, apparently.

DR KIM: Ethan's brother?

BETH: Yeah. I mean, I know people who live in glass nut houses shouldn't throw stones, but yeah, so Ethan thinks anyway.

DR KIM: Why?

BETH: He's found religion, apparently, the brother. Ethan's weirded out.

DR KIM: How do you feel?

BETH: About?

DR KIM: Finding religion.

BETH: Well, like I've said my mom's parents are from Belfast and my dad was a Palestinian from Jerusalem who came over in '48 when he was a baby, so they kind of came here to get away from religion. Freedom of religion I think pretty much meant freedom from religion for them.

DR KIM: Some people who've undergone something like you have are able to find faith quite healing.

BETH: That's what Ethan's brother did. He acquired it after...he was in 9/11.

DR KIM: Oh.

BETH: "Oh."(*Quick smile*) Ethan says he was in the second tower too. Forty-somethingth floor.

DR KIM: Have you met him yet?

BETH: No. Next week I will though. Him and his wife, who Ethan thinks is also not thrilled with the whole God thing either.

DR KIM: Have you thought about what it will be like to meet him?

BETH: Meaning?

DR KIM: Meaning—

BETH: You mean, will I wonder, did he see Alec? Was he next to him? Can he tell me if Alec was panicked? Am I going to wonder—did he try to help Alec? Did he push Alec out of his way so he could escape himself?

DR KIM: Do you find yourself asking that question?

BETH: I find myself asking that question about everyone. Even people I know weren't there.

DR KIM: Really?

BETH: Sometimes.

DR KIM: (*Pause*) Has Ethan told his family you lost someone on 9/11?

BETH: I'm not sure, actually. We don't—you know, we don't dwell on it.

DR KIM: I'm not suggesting you should.

BETH: Am I under some ethical obligation to tell everyone I meet? I mean, 'cos it's quite the fucking albatross, I've gotta tell ya. Because when you tell someone about it, they usually end up resenting the hell out of you.

DR KIM: You feel people resent you?

BETH: How could they not? I'm a walking reminder of the worst collective memory of their lives. How can you honestly expect people to ever get past that? They feel awful for me, of course, and they go out of their way to be kind—which in itself is usually a kind of contempt—but like all people you feel awful for, people start to wonder in a corner of their minds they don't even realize they've got why I haven't had the decency to just go away.

DR KIM: What about Ethan? Do you think he feels that way?

BETH: No. But, I mean, it's early yet; give him time.

(Blackout)

Scene Five

(An upscale bar in Manhattan. Happy Hour. JOSH waiting for ETHAN. ETHAN enters.)

ETHAN: Hey.

JOSH: Hey. I ordered your beer for you.

ETHAN: What a big brotherly thing to do So…what's up?

JOSH: Oh, you know.

(JOSH says a quick prayer before he drinks. ETHAN shifts about, embarrassed and awkward.)

ETHAN: See the game last night?

JOSH: No.

ETHAN: Smart move. Although I don't think what the Jets are doing can be considered anymore as "playing football". The fun in watching them is in figuring out what exactly they are doing—I mean it's something they're serious about, because, you know, they show up in uniform every week, but, I don't know. I don't know a lot about performance art, but some of the stuff the offensive line's doing I'm pretty sure is groundbreaking.

JOSH: Haven't really been following it.

ETHAN: Yeah. Gearing up for Mom's? Over the river and through the woods and shit?

JOSH: Actually, that's what I sort of wanted to talk to you about.

ETHAN: No no no no no. You cannot back out—I'm bringing someone and I need as many buffers as I can—

JOSH: No, no, I'm coming. It's that I need...I think it might get a little weird and you've always been better at dealing with Mom and so I wanted your take on how to handle some stuff.

ETHAN: Really? You think I'm better at dealing with Mom?

JOSH: I—yeah, of course. Better than me, I think, yeah.

ETHAN: Really it's Jessica who handles her best. Of course, she didn't grow up with her, so big advantage there, I'd think.

JOSH: The thing is though the weirdness will involve Jess. I think maybe we're getting divorced.

ETHAN: What the—shit. Why?

JOSH: A whole bunch of reasons, but most immediately because I'm going to move to Israel and she won't join me.

ETHAN: You can't...shit, why on earth are you...why the hell are you doing that?

JOSH: You honestly didn't think this might be coming?

ETHAN: It's beyond my ability to process...what the fuck, Josh? This is crazy.

JOSH: Yeah, well, I think you're crazy to want to stay here, but I don't think we're going to see eye to eye on this. You think I'm crazy, fine—so does Jess—you'll have a lot to chat about next week then.

ETHAN: But...can you, can you give me a reason?

JOSH: I can tell you why I don't want to stay here. Look around you—we're less than a mile from where the planes hit.

ETHAN: I know.

JOSH: Then look at everyone here, drinking and flirting and talking about the pitcher the fucking Yankees should go after and....I'm not saying there are people who aren't impacted—I'm talking about the...this sort of trademark American optimism...it's mindless, you know, the *way* the way we—we—com*mod*ified and— the way we—

ETHAN: Commodified? That must be quite the heavy load of bullshit you're carrying if you feel you need a word with that many letters to prop it up—

JOSH: Shut up for a second. I know I sound ridiculous sometimes, Ethan, I promise you I do know. It'd be great if you could find a way not remind me of it every chance you get. I'm trying to...I'm aware of how absurd I seem to most people. To you. Let's not talk about it, O K?

ETHAN: I'm sorry. It used to be part of the fun, though, you know? The little digs we'd—but you're right. But I do think if there's more—division in the country maybe nowadays it's because people are more engaged in the debate, you know, we're—

JOSH: What did you do on Memorial Day this year?

ETHAN: On Memorial Day?

JOSH: Yeah, I'm trying to flesh out your definition of "more engaged". The beach? A barbecue maybe? Some radio station counting down the hundred greatest albums of rock? In Israel, the television stations list the name and pictures of all the Israeli war dead. It takes a full day.

ETHAN: Have you visited?

JOSH: Israel?

ETHAN: Yes, Josh, fucking Israel. Have you actually bothered to visit the place before you go traipsing off to the Promised Land?

JOSH: I strike you as a traipser?

ETHAN: Off topic now.

JOSH: I went. Last month.

ETHAN: No you didn't.

JOSH: Yeah, like nine days.

ETHAN: I speak to you like twice a week, when could you have—

JOSH: You spoke to me when I was there. You called my cell.

ETHAN: Well, this is a whole new level of fucked up we've embarked on here.

JOSH: I didn't want to have to explain it to anyone… besides it would have looked weird that Jess wasn't there.

ETHAN: Yes, well…fine. So fine. Listen, it's not like I don't—I don't entirely disagree with you. About America. I'm not to be as political as you, but that—

JOSH: You're an American. To the rest of the world, that's the biggest political statement you can make. And that you don't get that, that no one here gets it or seems willing to accept the consequences of that…I don't know. That's why I'm leaving. Part of it anyway.

ETHAN: I don't know what to say to that; I don't.

JOSH: Then be smart and don't say anything.

ETHAN: No it's that…Jesus, I'm sorry Josh, but I think, you've managed to *romanticize* what's happened to you.

JOSH: *Romanticize*—fuck you, O K, Ethan?

ETHAN: No, I'm…I'm sorry; but these bastards who did it, when it boils down to it, they were just, just fucked up, fucking cruel hearted scum. It wasn't part of some intricate political web; it just gave these bastards an outlet. There's people who'll find an excuse to hurl rocks or grenades or airplanes at people no matter the political landscape. I mean it's nicer to think it's got to *do* with politics or religion or history, frankly, it's a kind of comfort because then A) maybe there's a solution to it and B) the killers and the victims can feel better about it all; it gives it a larger purpose somehow. But it's all a rationale.

JOSH: Wow. You actually took the time to rehearse a speech to give me.

ETHAN: No, no, I…a little.

JOSH: The A and B thing.

ETHAN: Too on the nose?

JOSH: But nice.

ETHAN: Thanks. Do you—seriously, do you see my point, though?

JOSH: Yes, I have to admit I do; I see it quite clearly. It's an incredibly dumb point, but I do see it. Maybe it would have a little more weight if the man talking to me about the, about all of this had an understanding of political or spiritual ideals that ran deeper than Tivoing episodes of *Frontline*. Maybe, but I doubt it. Maybe you *should* stick to talking about the Jets. *(Small smile)* That was the speech *I* rehearsed.

ETHAN: *(As honest a question as he's ever asked)* What happened, Josh? What's happening?

JOSH: *(Tries for a moment to give an answer)* What can I...

(ETHAN and JOSH both seem to sense the futility; they move on.)

JOSH: I want your help getting through Thanksgiving, you know, and I wanted you to know why it's liable to be really stressful for Jess and me. That's why I brought all this up. I mean, I can't imagine I'm going to tell Mom that day, but...*you* don't think I should do it before, do you?

ETHAN: I think it's a bad idea to tell Mom anything. Ever. About anything. I've lied to her about weather forecasts. Dad's been dead, what, twenty years, and if she hadn't found the body, I'd still not tell her about that. So.

JOSH: Yeah. *(Pause)* So. This girl, this woman, Beth? Getting pretty serious, huh?

ETHAN: Oh, I don't—I'm like the world's worst judge of that, I...I don't know. Her uh...she's um.

JOSH: What? She's what?

ETHAN: Hmm? Nothing—she's nice, I was gonna say, but then I realized how stupid that sounded.

JOSH: Oh. Well. That's not stupid. That's a lot. Although I get the feeling maybe that could be Ethanspeak for "I really enjoy banging her."

ETHAN: *(Not insulted)* Funny you should mention that. We haven't even yet.

JOSH: What do you mean you haven't even? Even what? Slept with her?

ETHAN: *(Almost proud)* Yep.

JOSH: You? Almost three months and no— you do realize "sleep with" for most people is a euphemism for sex and not, you know, three-way sex.

ETHAN: *(Laughing)* Yes.

JOSH: Wow. I'm...I'm oddly impressed.

ETHAN: You know what? Me too. I kind of wonder if for me it's maybe like the reverse of what it is for most people: maybe it's a sign I'm really, I don't know.

JOSH: Serious about her?

ETHAN: I don't know. Maybe.

JOSH: So this *is* serious—

ETHAN: No, no, I don't know. You know me.

JOSH: Well—serious for you. I mean we might actually *meet* her. That's like—for you—like getting engaged.

ETHAN: *(Playful)* Fuck off.

JOSH: Oh, I'm so sorry; I *do* apologize. So I take it you've *stopped* boffing the receptionist at your office, then, if this is so special.

(ETHAN smiles sheepishly.)

JOSH: I see, I see, yes, you're right, I do apologize.

ETHAN: Well, you know, Beth and I aren't like en*gaged* or anything, you know?

JOSH: Although the re*cept*ionist is, if I recall.

ETHAN: Hey, in this topsy-turvy world of ours, I try not to judge.

JOSH: You are a dick.

ETHAN: I know, I know. I do kind of like this one, though.

JOSH: Well, I'm glad then. Another beer?

ETHAN: Are you?

JOSH: Sure.

ETHAN: All right. Cool. I got it. *(He goes to bar.)*

(Lights fade.)

Scene Six

(We see BETH talking to ALEC—the audience of course assumes at first that this is DR KIM—this is fine—in fact, good—and of course it isn't really ALEC either—it is simply BETH's projection of him—BETH harbors no illusions about this, but it doesn't diminish him in her mind.)

BETH: I stopped taking my pills.

ALEC: Why?

BETH: I think it was doing more harm than good.

ALEC: Meaning?

BETH: Well, I'm still—how do I put it—fucked up.

ALEC: And you think that's the pills?

BETH: No but they're not—um…defuckifying me, shall we say; so why put up with the side effects?

ALEC: What are your side effects?

BETH: Well, um, gee, my therapist appears to me as my dead husband.

ALEC: That's not a side effect.

BETH: Yeah, but it hasn't stopped.

ALEC: A pill's not going to stop that.

BETH: That your diagnosis?

ALEC: I'm just saying.

BETH: And then there's this.

ALEC: This?

BETH: This shit.

ALEC: This shit?

BETH: This seeing you randomly now shit. Having you pop up out of the blue, free form. I mean, I'm now officially a full blown delusional. I'm not seeing you as someone else.

ALEC: I gotta ask—you think that's worse?

BETH: I don't know, Alec, I don't have a fucking chart on this—I'm pretty sure it's not better—it's not a question of, a question of worse. It's more. *(Tears in spite of herself)* More of this shit. I'm never going to get past this.

ALEC: You're not delusional.

BETH: That's a little self-serving coming from a delusion.

ALEC: You don't think I'm real. If you were introducing me to people, then I'd start worrying.

BETH: Then you'd worry? I think that ship's sailed, no?

ALEC: Well…you've always been very creative. That's all this is.

BETH: No it's not.

ALEC: Well. You should call Doctor Kim.

BETH: I'm not calling her on Thanksgiving.

ALEC: You should tell her about us.

BETH: Yeah.

ALEC: I mean, about our last—

BETH: Yeah, I know.

ALEC: *(Over "I know")* Chat.

BETH: Chat? Fuck you.

ALEC: It's so not fair of you to get pissy over my word choice when you're the one who chooses them.

BETH: *(Trying to gather herself)* Right. O K. Right—I—I gotta— Ethan's picking me up in a minute.

ALEC: Yeah.

BETH: I'm meeting his family.

ALEC: Like I don't know that.

BETH: Alec—I…Jesus, you look so good.

ALEC: Well, you've spruced me up a bit. I'm sort of idealized. Which I'm completely fine with, by the way.

BETH: It's nice I remember you that way though, right? That's something.

ALEC: Well, that's because of the guilt.

BETH: Probably.

ALEC: *(Admires himself in mirror)* Still, nice job. If I existed, I'd be getting a lot of play.

BETH: I got your sense of humor about right, though.

ALEC: Yeah. That's key.

BETH: Absolutely. Biggest part of your charm.

ALEC: Thank you. I was charming.

BETH: Endlessly.

ALEC: No. Not endlessly.

BETH: No.

ALEC: But I was charming. *(Not a plea or outburst of any sort—a genuine question)* How in the world could you have told me you were leaving me?

BETH: I don't know.

ALEC: But you did.

BETH: Yeah.

ALEC: And I cried all night. You fell asleep to my sniffling.

BETH: And when I woke up you'd gone to work.

ALEC: I did. And then…

BETH: And then…here we are.

ALEC: Here we are.

(Apartment intercom buzzes.)

ALEC: Ride's here.

(Blackout)

Scene Seven

(The kitchen of RACHEL's *home in Jericho, Long Island. An impressive stack of Thanksgiving food in catering containers stands on the kitchen table.* RACHEL *and* JESSICA *are taking inventory.* JESSICA *is drinking a glass of wine.)*

RACHEL: I ordered too much.

JESSICA: No, it just *looks* like a lot.

RACHEL: It *is* a lot; too much maybe.

JESSICA: No, it's a lot, but that's what you want at Thanksgiving, no?

RACHEL: I don't know—yes, but—I can't eat all these leftovers. The thing is, I don't really like turkey. You'll take the leftovers.

JESSICA: Well, we'll take some.

RACHEL: Don't worry, they're kosher, Josh'll be ok with it.

JESSICA: No, that isn't why I—I mean, Ethan'll want some to, no?

RACHEL: Yeah, I hope. And the girl, she can take some too.

JESSICA: Yeah; good. *(Small pause)*

RACHEL: Do we *like* her?

JESSICA: *(Small laugh)* Um, I don't know…*do* we?

RACHEL: *(Shrugs)* Who knows, right? She seems nice, I think. Don't you think? She seems nice?

JESSICA: Well, I've known her for about a half an hour, twenty minutes of which she's been in another room, but yeah, she does. Where *are* they, actually?

RACHEL: Ethan took her for a walk. Showing her the neighborhood.

JESSICA: It's twenty-five degrees out.

(RACHEL shrugs in agreement.)

JESSICA: Still, that's cute actually. The stage they're at, the first blush, the more uncomfortable something is, the more romantic.

RACHEL: I suppose. Josh watching the football game?

JESSICA: No, C N N, there was a bomber on a bus in Tel Aviv.

RACHEL: Ah. *(Pause)* When Ethan gets back they'll watch the game, maybe.

JESSICA: This is a lot. It seems like more than last year, somehow.

RACHEL: That's what I was thinking. But it's not. I ordered off the receipt from last year.

JESSICA: Well, better to have and not need than need and not have, as my grandmother used to say.

(JOSH *enters.*)

JOSH: Seventeen dead.

JESSICA: That's awful.

JOSH: Yeah.

(*Pause*)

RACHEL: I ordered too much I think.

JOSH: Hmm?

JESSICA: Your mother's worried she ordered too much food.

JOSH: Oh.

JESSICA: And I was saying it's Thanksgiving, you're supposed to have a lot.

JOSH: Mm-hmm.

RACHEL: Ethan still out with, with um, Beth?

JOSH: Dunno.

RACHEL: Well, while I've got you two here, let me ask you about my idea.

JESSICA: What idea?

RACHEL: Well, it's… (*To* JOSH) I spoke to your aunt.

JOSH: Helen?

RACHEL: Who else?

JESSICA: How is she?

RACHEL: Who knows—she's in Florida—all you ever hear from her is weather reports. But she's been encouraging me to come down there with her. To live.

JESSICA: Yeah?

RACHEL: At least part of the year, yeah. The winter. With the snow and everything by myself, it's getting to be too much.

JOSH: You have a guy who plows the driveway for you, right?

RACHEL: Yeah, but that's not—that's not it. I get…it's been a little lonely here. Not that you should have to visit me all the time. Or once every couple weeks, even. But here—here's my idea.

JOSH: O K.

RACHEL: So. I sell you this house—for two-thirds the value—I give half of what you pay me to Ethan so he gets something too and I get a condo down there. In Helen's building. And you keep the guest room for me to visit up in the summer. It'd be a steal for you. And a house. Build up some equity instead of just paying rent all the time.

JOSH: Well, Mom, we…we like living in the city.

RACHEL: Yes, but you used to love living in Jericho, too. When you and Ethan were boys.

JOSH: Yes, when we were boys.

RACHEL: But to raise a family—that's why I thought you two instead of Ethan. So? What do we think? Win-win, as they say, I think.

JESSICA: Well, it's a…it's a very generous offer, Rachel.

JOSH: Yes.

RACHEL: Yes, yes, I know. Forget generous. What do you *think*?

JOSH: It's a lot to think about, Mom.

JESSICA: It *is* a lot to think about it. In a good way.

RACHEL: I know. But you know sometimes it's possible to over think things.

JESSICA: Yes.

RACHEL: The city's wonderful, don't get me wrong, but to raise a family?

JOSH: Mom…

JESSICA: It's not unheard of.

RACHEL: I mean, if you're *planning* on children at some point.

JOSH: Why are we talking about *this* now?

RACHEL: So I can't mention the *possibility* of children? Like it's a calamity? When you first got married it's all you two talked about. Yes, yes sorry. Sorry I—it's the—what's the expression, the elephant in the room.

JESSICA: Womb.

JOSH: *(To Jessica: "Stop encouraging her")* Can we not?

RACHEL: O K, well…you two think about it, no rush.

JESSICA: Thank you Rachel. It's a very nice—it's a terrific gesture, right Josh?

JOSH: It's very…yes, thanks Mom.

RACHEL: Well, I want you to be happy and…anyway, I was hoping maybe we could think about doing it by January.

JESSICA: Interesting definition of "no rush".

RACHEL: Is that too soon?

JOSH: No, Ma, let's…just we need to think about it a little.

RACHEL: Fine, fine. Not today; not today at all. Let's just enjoy today. And try to make a dent in this food. *(She rather suddenly and conspicuously, exits.)*

JOSH: Where are you going, Mom?

RACHEL: *(Offstage)* Upstairs for a minute. Just, I have to… *(She doesn't finish the sentence.)*

JESSICA: Exit Rachel, suspiciously. *(Pause)* Well, good thing *that* wasn't awkward, huh?

JOSH: What the hell was that?

JESSICA: She wants to move. That's life, right? I mean she's still fairly young—hell in your Aunt Helen's condo she'd be like jailbait. And maybe…maybe she feels trapped by this place. She *is* kind of isolated out here, most of her friends have moved. I think she was trying to be helpful, too.

JOSH: Uh-huh.

JESSICA: I mean, economically, it make a lot of sense.

JOSH: Yeah.

JESSICA: I mean, if we still liked each other, it would be great, actually.

JOSH: *(With a real anger that takes both of them by surprise)* Stop *say*ing shit like that.

JESSICA: Well, it's true.

JOSH: No, it's not. It's not a question of *liking* each other.

JESSICA: Of course it is.

JOSH: Do you really think that? Do you really think that all of this has happened because we've stopped *liking* each other?

JESSICA: No. I think it's because you stopped liking me.

JOSH: That's not true. I still like you.

JESSICA: Please don't.

JOSH: Don't what?

JESSICA: Try to be nice to me. It's cruel.

JOSH: It's not that I don't like you. It's…I…

JESSICA: No one's expecting you to get past what happened. How can you if you keep shutting me out? What's the point of us if I can't help you get past it?

JOSH: That's not what I'm talking about. That's not...

JESSICA: What?

JOSH: That's not what I can't get past.

JESSICA: Well then, as usual, we're not talking about the same thing.

JOSH: No.

(Pause)

JESSICA: Ah...it's me you can't get past.

JOSH: Not you, no...

JESSICA: Then what? What, finally?

JOSH: It's...I don't know.*(Hoping to end the discussion)* I don't want to talk about it. Not here.

JESSICA: Of course not.

JOSH: Not here.

JESSICA: Then where? At home? You'll talk to me about it there? No you won't, Josh, you know you won't. Why is it you're eager to talk about the plight of every Jew in the world except the two of us?

JOSH: It's not you I don't like, Jessica. Or love for that matter. It's just...

JESSICA: What? What, goddammit?

JOSH: The life you want to lead.

JESSICA: Well, is that all? You don't hate me, just my life; just everything *about* me. That is...that is one *thin* fucking sliver of a distinction to support the weight of our marriage with, don't you think?

JOSH: Yeah

Pause.

JESSICA: Well then, what else is there to say, eh?

(JESSICA *exits, taking a bottle of wine with her.* JOSH *sits at the table.* BETH *and* ETHAN *enter.*)

ETHAN: Hey.

JOSH: Hey.

BETH: Ethan was showing me around your old neighborhood.

JOSH: Ah. See anything interesting?

BETH: Oh yeah, it's a very nice place—you guys had a nice community to grow up in.

JOSH: *(Ignoring her)* Ethan, let me—did—did you tell Mom?

ETHAN: About?

JOSH: About…about what I told you about. Last week.

ETHAN: You mean about…about you and—

JOSH: Yes.

ETHAN: No.

JOSH: No?

ETHAN: No, what am I, *lying* to you about this? No.

JOSH: You didn't.

ETHAN: What did I just say?

JOSH: Mm-hmm.

ETHAN: Hey, goddammit, don't "Mm-hmm" me like that. Jesus. I mean, just because you've turned into Super Jew doesn't give you the right to go around all assholier than thou.

JOSH: Don't say Jew like that.

ETHAN: Like *what*?

JOSH: Like it's an insult.

ETHAN: Well, I...well...don't fucking call me a liar.

JOSH: Has she talked to you ?

ETHAN: About?

JOSH: Her plan.

ETHAN: No. What plan?

JOSH: She wants to sell the house to Jess and me for two-thirds the value and give you half the money.

ETHAN: Oh. Why?

JOSH: She thinks she wants to move to Florida. With Helen. Says she's alone here.

ETHAN: Oh. Well, O K.

JOSH: No Ethan, it's not O K, for reasons that should be obv—I thought it was an attempt of hers to get Jess and me...anyway, I don't wanna go into it now, but, if she mentions anything to you, be sort of, I don't know, vague but pleasant, maybe.

ETHAN: When I am ever not that way with Mom?

JOSH: Right.

ETHAN: And why do you think I'd tell her about you and—when do I tell Mom anything?

JOSH: Well, normally you don't, no.

ETHAN: Exactly; thank you.

JOSH: But I'm sure you've all talked about me recently; I mean... (To BETH) I mean Ethan's told you about me, right? That I'm (sotto voce) moving to Israel, which he feels is crazy, right?

BETH: Well, he did tell me something about that, yeah—not the you being crazy part—and that you went there recently.

JOSH: He hasn't said how he thinks it's crazy?

ETHAN: Hey, Josh—

BETH: I think that's maybe a bit far; I think he's a little…puzzled.

JOSH: And you no doubt find it puzzling, too. Wanting to leave a "nice community" like this.

BETH: No, I wouldn't say that. I don't know. Actually, I've sometimes thought of going, too.

JOSH: Really?

BETH: Yeah, not a lot, but…my grandparents were Palestinian. My dad, too, but he came over when he was a baby.

JOSH: Oh.

BETH: Yeah. *(Smiles)* Sorry you asked, now, huh?

(Blackout)

END OF ACT ONE

ACT TWO

Scene One

(The stage is separated into three sections, demarcated by light and shadow: RACHEL's *living room area, presently in black, which contains* JESSICA; RACHEL's *bathroom, whose lights are the first to come up, which contains* BETH *and* ALEC—BETH *looking into the mirror,* ALEC *seated on the edge of the tub or toilet; and* RACHEL's *kitchen, which holds* ETHAN *and* RACHEL. *The lights should come up in each section as each couple begins their dialogue. Sometimes the dialogue is essentially simultaneous and therefore almost overlaps.)*

BETH: *(Into the mirror and therefore to us: occasionally distracted from us by* ALEC*)* So. So far: not as bad as I'd have thought. The tension part of it, I mean. Considering my little moment with Josh, *and* it's obvious he and his wife aren't hitting it off. I mean, Ethan told me they might be splitting up, so maybe it's just obvious to me, but still. And the mother's...I don't know. Slightly nervous vibe from her, actually. Which is of course odd because it should be me who's...but maybe I'm projecting.

ALEC: You're quite good at that.

BETH: Or maybe because she's nervous about bringing up selling the house.

ETHAN: Selling the house, huh?

RACHEL: Yes. What do you think, sweetie?

ETHAN: Well I...wow.

RACHEL: Why is that such a big—your brother had the same reaction.

ETHAN: Well, I don't know, it isn't I guess.

BETH: Which I think would be very tough to bring up to them; I mean, they grew up here.

(Lights dim slightly on BETH *and* ALEC.)

ETHAN: Except that we grew up here.

RACHEL: I understand that, Ethan. I raised my family here. But...I'm, I'm not a curator, this isn't a museum.

ETHAN: I know.

RACHEL: I have to live here. Alone. Which I'm sick to death of, by the way, living alone, with you and Josh visiting me whenever you can be bothered.

ETHAN: *(Not without affection)* You know Mom, I've always been a little in awe of your ability to take any conversation, any strand of anything, like our chat now about, you know, real estate, and make it into an instrument of guilt.

RACHEL: If you feel guilty every time you talk to me, maybe that says more about you than me, no?

ETHAN: Good job, Ma, well done, you're endlessly resourceful with it—you're the MacGyver of guilt.

RACHEL: I have no idea what that means but I'm sure you're over exaggerating.

ETHAN: As opposed to exaggerating just the right amount.

RACHEL: Fine, Mister Sarcasm, tell Beth dinner's ready.

BETH: *(Lights back up to full strength)* But yet, despite the occasional signal that something's up...

RACHEL: She's in the bathroom.

BETH: …it seems all right.

RACHEL: She's been in there for a while, is she all right?

BETH: Not that I'm the best judge of that.

ALEC: True.

ETHAN: I'm sure she's fine, probably just stopping to admire—as we all have—your impressive collection of fine decorative soaps.

BETH: I haven't been…what Doctor Kim would call "really present" most of the day. Ethan took me on tour of his neighborhood and I can't remember a thing.

ALEC: Maybe it's because you stopped your pills.

BETH: You know, I'm not so round-the-bend crazy that I can't go off them for a few days without losing it completely.

ALEC: Who are you trying to convince, yourself or the hallucination you're talking to in your boyfriend's mother's bathroom?

ETHAN: *(Knocks on the door)* Beth?

BETH: *(A response to both* ALEC *and* ETHAN*)* Yeah.

ETHAN: You O K?

BETH: Yeah, sorry, be out in a sec.

ALEC: Poor Ethan.

ETHAN: O K, we're sitting down to eat in a minute.

BETH: O K. *(Back to us—she turns to* ALEC *as if she's about to object to what he's said, then admits it to herself.)* Poor Ethan. I really do…care for him; he's smart and sweet and funny. But I'm not…I can't stay connected to anyone. Anyone. Or anyplace. Least of all myself. And I'd love to be able to blame this on…what happened. But all that did, honestly, is cement it. I've been this way for…a long time. Connect for a while and then, without realizing it, drift away. *(Pause)* Alec used to catch me doing it.

ALEC: I could always tell.

BETH: Yes.

ALEC: It's why you were drawn to me in the first place.

BETH: I know.

ALEC: You'd hoped—

BETH: I know what I'd hoped.

ALEC: Sorry.

BETH: I'd hoped someone seeing me do it would stop me from doing it to them. But of course, it just made it…sadder.

ALEC: You were present when you got back from your walk, though. When you were talking to Josh.

(JOSH enters the kitchen area with ETHAN and RACHEL.)

RACHEL: Josh, sweetie, go get Jessica; it's almost time to eat.

JOSH: K.

(As JOSH crosses to JESSICA's part of the stage, the kitchen area goes black.)

BETH: He just seems so…unrelenting. I don't know how people live like that.

ALEC: Who, Josh? Like what?

BETH: Like everything's a challenge. Exhausting.

ALEC: Yes, if only people could find a way to cope like you have. Why are you wasting Ethan's time?

BETH: I'm not.

ALEC: Or yours?

BETH: I am trying, I'm trying to…

ALEC: Ultimately it's cruel, what you're doing to him.

BETH: (*During the course of these lines the lights dim on* ALEC *until, by the end of these lines, he can no longer be seen*) No, it's not, I'm…it's up to me to—I have to—I am going out there, with him with this sweet man and his fucked up brother and I am going to be sweet and charming and, and, *have a good time*, and make Ethan fall in love with me and I am going let myself fall in love with him and then we are going to go home—a little drunk hopefully—and we're going to make love and spend all the next day in bed and I am going to be honest and good to him and I am going to let him be those things to me. It's not my fault we drifted. Or that you went to work that day. O K. O K. O K.

(*Lights fade on* BETH *and the bathroom area goes black as the lights rise on the living room area with* JESSICA *and* JOSH.)

JOSH: Jess.

JESSICA: What?

JOSH: (*Noticing drink in her hand and her slightly different manner*) Are you drinking?

JESSICA: A little. Do you disapprove? Branching into Puritanism now, too? Or perhaps Islam? I think you're better off sticking to one set of fundamentalist beliefs at a time.

JOSH: I just wanted to know if you were, I don't know…drunk.

JESSICA: A little, I think, but on the other hand, I just breezed through the phrase "fundamentalist beliefs" pretty crisply so I think you could maybe lighten up a little.

JOSH: Fine, whatever, fine. Dinner's about to be served. And by the way, speaking of Islam, ready for this? She's Palestinian.

JESSICA: Who?

JOSH: Beth.

JESSICA: Beth?

JOSH: Yes.

JESSICA: *(Reflects on this)* Is she an albino?

JOSH: No, she's only half. The other half's Irish, I think.

JESSICA: Oh. So?

JOSH: So? Don't you think it's a little odd Ethan never mentioned that?

JESSICA: *(Bursts out laughing)* Are you kidding? Jesus, are you—would *you* mention that to you?

JOSH: It's the principle of the—

JESSICA: The principle? What fucked up racist principle would that be? And since when's your brother required to submit geneology profiles of people he's sleeping with?

JOSH: That's not what I'm—I'm not racist.

JESSICA: No? Then what? Worried she's here to blow us up? She's in the bathroom now? I can sneak in and see if she's got any explosives strapped to her.

JOSH: That's not what I mean, and you know it's not what I mean. You're deliberately twisting this to make into a race thing, it's the…you're right, let's not do it here.

JESSICA: There's nothing to do, Josh. It's done. We're getting divorced. I *need* to divorce you—it's clear now—to divorce myself from you.

JOSH: If that's what you need.

JESSICA: Oh, aren't you big? What a *mensch* you are. Don't you fucking act like that's not what you want. Like it's not what you've been longing to hear from me for months now so you can go off to the West Bank with a clear conscience.

JOSH: That's not true.

JESSICA: It's not even enough to divorce you any more, it's too late for that even, somehow. You know what you've done to me? You've done it—the exact opposite of what you'd hoped, by the way, so I guess I should take a little consolation in that. For the first time in my life, you've made me wish I weren't Jewish.

JOSH: What are you talking about?

JESSICA: It's true, I wish I were Catholic, Josh, I do, I pray to a great big blond-haired, small-nosed Goyish God to make me a Catholic just long enough for me to get an *annulment*. What a wonderful thing that must be. To annul—to erase somebody like that.

JOSH: It's really unimpressive of you in this moment, in this sad moment, to be so intent on trying to hurt me. It's childish.

JESSICA: I'm only telling you the truth. What's in my heart. That's all you've been doing to me, right? You know…Josh, I have to tell you…and I swore I never would—but in dark little moments, for months now, I've found myself fantasizing what it would be like if you'd been killed with everyone else that day. At first, it was almost subliminal, you know—too ashamed to stay in my mind for long. But then—at some point— and not when you became distant and not when you stopped sleeping with me—not then—only *after* that, only after it became clear that those things were happening not because of what happened to you, but because of who I was, only when you became visibly *contemptuous* of me, of us, only after *that* settled around our apartment like all that grey dust did those first few weeks, that's when I couldn't help wondering what it would've been like if I could have just…been allowed to mourn you publicly, once and for all, when the rest of the civilized world was grieving, too. Instead of what I ended up doing—mourning you privately every day since then. It's the opposite of being haunted. Everyone can see you, but I'm the only one who knows you're not there. That everything I loved, your friends and family knew of you, is gone. What I'm saying is, I guess, is for what you've done to us, how you've treated me, you might as well be dead.

(We hear RACHEL's *voice off stage.)*

RACHEL: Josh, Jessica, come on already; it's dinner.

(Blackout)

Scene Two

(The dinner table RACHEL, JESSICA, ETHAN, BETH *and* JOSH. *It's about twenty minutes or so into the meal— everyone's had enough time to eat at least one course— the conversation has been a little strained, as* JESSICA *is now visibly drunk—and this is not a situation they've encountered before.* JOSH *seems more detached and laconic than ever, apart from an occasional flash of anger and disgust racing across his face. But the others press ahead valiantly.)*

BETH: Everything is delicious.

RACHEL: Well have some more.

BETH: Oh no, I'm stuffed.

RACHEL: Oh, that's crazy, you've barely eaten a thing.

BETH: God, no, are you kidding?

RACHEL: Eat some more stuffing.

BETH: Well, a—a dollop. A half a dollop, really. Half a metric dollop.

RACHEL: I'm sorry?

BETH: Nothing, never mind, just a little bit, please.

ETHAN: There's no such thing as "just a little bit" of food when my mother's serving.

RACHEL: Well, it's Thanksgiving, there shouldn't be any such thing, right?

ETHAN: It's an oxymoron, like jumbo shrimp or Fox News. This is great stuff, Ma, I love the potatoes—we had these last year, right? The dinner last year?

JESSICA: Last supper.

RACHEL: What, honey?

JOSH: It's—she's—she was making a joke. She's had a little bit too much wine.

JESSICA: I'm a big girl, can handle myself.

RACHEL: Everything's the same as last year, absolutely everything.

(JESSICA *half snorts a laugh at this.*)

ETHAN: Weren't they good Josh? The potatoes?

JOSH: Yeah.

JESSICA: I love red potatoes. I love them mashed like this. Or roasted.

BETH: They're great.

JESSICA: I haven't made them for so long though, because Josh hates roasted potatoes.

JOSH: I like them mashed.

JESSICA: Yes, but they're too fattening to eat them mashed all the time. I love like, roasted chicken with roasted potatoes but I haven't made it for so long because he hates it. There's a lot of food I've stopped making just because Josh doesn't like it.

JOSH: How did saying I like the potatoes turn into an attack on me?

JESSICA: Awww.

BETH: I know what you're saying, though, Jessica, I do. When you're married to someone you end up adopting their habits. Alec used to hate to eat anything tomatoey—so after a while I just stopped eating it myself—I only recently rediscovered it—I can't believe I went so long without it.

RACHEL: Alec was...I'm sorry, who was Alec?

(ALEC now appears—it should be sudden but not overly dramatic—he should simply be there.)

ALEC: Why would you bring me into this?

BETH: Oh, um, he was my—sorry, yeah—my husband.

ALEC: Jesus.

RACHEL: Oh, you were—

ETHAN: Beth's husband died in 9/11.

ALEC: And cue the awkward silence.

(JESSICA downs her glass of wine. ETHAN, too, takes a rather large gulp of his)

ALEC: Nice work; you've just invented the world's most depressing drinking game.

JOSH: What?

RACHEL: Oh...I'm...so sorry.

BETH: Thank you.

JOSH: World Trade Center?

BETH: Yes. I hear that you were there, too.

JOSH: Is that what you heard?

ALEC: Oh Christ. And I *liked* tomatoes—they just made my lips puff up—I looked like a deranged Renee Zelwegger.

RACHEL: It was a terrible, terrible, time for everyone.

ETHAN: Mom—

BETH: Yes.

RACHEL: Not that I need to tell—well, let's not—I'm sorry.

BETH: It's really, no—thank you. I think I *will* have a little more potatoes, now that we were talking about them.

ALEC: Yes, the carbs will save you.

BETH: Dinner really is terrific.

RACHEL: Oh well, thanks, yes, thanks, we like these caterers a lot, don't we?

ETHAN: Yeah.

BETH: How long have you used these people?

RACHEL: This is only the second year, actually. After the boys' father died…he died very young, too, I mean, I—anyway—I soldiered on for a few years but my heart wasn't in it and of course God forbid the boys show any appreciation for my efforts .

ETHAN: Mom.

RACHEL: I know. I should just be grateful for your company. Which is maybe the same attitude that has you going through girlfriends like Kleenex, but of course I'm only the your widowed mother, what do I know?

ETHAN: Ma.

RACHEL: Not that we don't all have high hopes for you Beth; you seem very lovely so far.

ETHAN: Nice save, Mom.

BETH: *(More amused than anything else)* Um, thanks, Mrs Harkman.

RACHEL: See? So polite, this one. Call me Rachel, please. So anyway, after my sister Helen moved to Florida we started ordering from places, but I think this is the best one, don't you agree?

ETHAN: Yeah, definitely.

RACHEL: I think we'll be going back to them next year, right?

JESSICA: Depends who's still here.

RACHEL: Well—I mean, yes, but, I'll be up for holidays and things like that. Unless everyone wants to come down to me.

JESSICA: That'll be a long trip for some of us.

RACHEL: No, it's only a couple of hours.

JOSH: Let's not talk about next year, please.

JESSICA: None of your business anymore, what I talk about. So, Beth, you're Palestinian, eh?

RACHEL: Really?

ETHAN: So what?

JESSICA: Josh didn't tell you, Rachel? He practically tripped over himself running to tell me.

ETHAN: What the hell, Josh?

ALEC: Oh, this is so cool.

BETH: God.

JESSICA: So. Palestinian. *That's* pretty fucked up, huh? How's that working out for you?

ETHAN: What the hell is—

BETH: Well it's no big deal, I'm, I mean, um, my Dad was born there is really the whole connection with it.

RACHEL: Oh. Well, that's O K.

ETHAN: Mom.

RACHEL: Oh she knows I didn't mean it like that.

BETH: It's O K, really. *(To* ETHAN*)* Really. Could I have the turkey, Josh?

*(*JOSH *hands the platter to* BETH*.)*

JESSICA: So you don't, you don't um…feel especially connected to it? I don't care one way or another you understand, it's just my—for lack of a better word—husband, you see, has developed a strong affinity for your dad's old neck of the woods.

RACHEL: What's going on here? What's the matter with you, Jessica?

JESSICA: Well, that's Josh's area of expertise—ask your son what's the matter with me—or any of you—he will have an endless catalogue of our failings as Jews or Americans or, or mammals.

ALEC: I admit it—this is way more fun than Thanksgiving at my folks house would've been.

RACHEL: Sweetheart, Jessica, honey, why don't—

JOSH: This won't work. You can't bait me.

JESSICA: Bait you? Are you kidding? Are you f—bait you for what? *(Real anger)* For *what*?!? What do you think can you offer me? What do you have to give besides contempt? Another of your endless lectures about history and the Jews or American foreign policy and the last days of Rome? Maybe I'm being selfish again, though Josh, you're right, you're right as always. Why be selfish, why not treat everyone else to a taste of your disdain? Talk about how shallow and naïve our lives are. Give `em the ol' firebrand New Zionist

Rhetoric, you know— "Foreskin and seven years ago…"

RACHEL: Jessica.

ETHAN: He lectures me, too.

JESSICA: Has he hit you with the one about Jews who marry or (*Glancing at* BETH) date out of the religion are essentially doing the same thing to the Jews as the Nazis?

JOSH: If you're trying to embarrass or hurt me you've hit me in the wrong spot– I am not going to apologize for my beliefs. To be a Jew is to be constantly attacked.

ETHAN: Oh please—

JOSH: Please?

JESSICA: No one's attacking Jews, we're attacking *you*— there *is* a difference. Have you really been listening to yourself all this time? I mean I understand why you have to make all these speeches, all these judgments, I understand it's your mind just trying to talk over your, your guilt. I get that, but I wonder sometimes if you do.

JOSH: (*Over "sometimes if you do."*) Stop your psychobabble—talk about superstition, that's your super—explain everything away with—

JESSICA: (*Over "explain everything away with"*) Because what else could drown out that guilt that, that—

RACHEL: Guilt, Jessica, Josh doesn't have anything to be—

JOSH: (*"Josh doesn't have anything to be—"*) No! Don't you diminish, don't you—

JESSICA: What else could drown out that epic guilt, the guilt you feel other than by making everyone else just as flawed, come up just as short?

RACHEL: Jessica, what are you talking-

ETHAN: Call me a fucking Nazi. *(Standing now and gesturing to* BETH*)* Let's go, let's get going, sorry Mom.

RACHEL: Oh, Ethan, no no. Josh!

ALEC: No—we can't go *now.*

JOSH: She's distorting, she's—

JESSICA: If only I were, you should hear, hear the noise he has to, he has to keep vomiting up to drown out the—

ETHAN: I know.

JESSICA: No you don't, you don't know *why* he's become—

JOSH: Stop it! That is *not* what this is, stop trying to diminish it—I didn't call you a Nazi, of course I don't think you're a—she's distorting , of course—but the fact is, the fact is we're breeding ourselves out of existence.

ETHAN: Anything that means we can't separate ourselves anymore is O K by me.

JOSH: Aw gee wiz, Ethan that's inspiring, very John-Lennon— "imagine all the people" of you. "Anything that means we can't separate ourselves" —this is what I'm talking about—what blithe little American bubble are you still floating around in that allows you to actually think that they'd ever let you forget you're a Jew to begin with?

ETHAN: They?

JOSH: Of course, goddammit, of course they! Dammit! I mean to be *naïve* about that, in this day and age is, is nothing short of criminal. I mean, to be Jewish and—

JESSICA: You don't get to tell us what it means to be Jewish! What I am, what that means to me is mine, ok?

JOSH: No, Jessica, it isn't, you see? You're actually part of a community.

JESSICA: I am part of my family.

JOSH: Who are *also* part of this community, whether they realize it or not.

ETHAN: Oh my God, just because we haven't all swallowed the kosher Kool Aid like you have doesn't mean we-

RACHEL: *(Puzzled)* What?

JOSH: *(Incensed)* What? Fuck you, Ethan! Fuck you and your, your fucking *irony*.

RACHEL: Josh!

JOSH: You know, Ethan, you and—and my *wife*—can be glib and, and ur*bane* about all you want, but the truth of it is you separate yourself from your group—

ETHAN: Our group?

JOSH: Your *community*—you do that and you've got nothing to do but to, to *stew* in your own psy*chology* and it hollows you out; it absolutely hollows you—

JESSICA: Don't you *dare* tell me I'm not connected to a— I have a community.

JOSH: We were never part of a community. Demographic, yes.

(JESSICA jumps across the table and tackles JOSH. She punches him and pulls at him as RACHEL screams "Jessica, Jessica!" while ETHAN screams "Shit!" and tries to pry them apart.)

JESSICA: I HATE YOU, I FUCKING HATE YOU, you fucking you KILLED us, killed my *LIFE*, you let us fucking die, too, you killer, fucking murderer, You fucking finished the job for them, you fucking accomplice! MURDERER!

(JESSICA *rips* JOSH's *yarmulke off and throws it to the ground.* ETHAN *finally pulls her off of* JOSH. JOSH *picks it up, dusts it off, kisses it, and places it again on his head.*)

JESSICA: I belonged, I belonged! To you.

RACHEL: Oh Jessica, sweetheart, it's O K, it's O—things will get better, I promise you, I promise you, when you move here, you'll slow down, you'll—

JESSICA: Oh, God, Rachel, we're not moving into this *house*, my God, where *are* you? Where have you been? We're not moving anywhere together. Josh wants to get the hell away from me—and all of you—as quickly as possible.

RACHEL: What are you talking—

JESSICA: He's leaving us. All of us. "Next year in Jerusalem." He's not here anymore. The little boy who swam in your backyard, the man who carried me piggyback across that muddy field sophomore year at the Grateful Dead show so my sneakers would... would stay white...he's gone. He's gone. He killed him. We're getting divorced.

RACHEL: Oh my God, Jessica.

ETHAN: It's O K, Mom.

RACHEL: No, it's not, it's terrible. We can't fly apart like this. A family doesn't, doesn't: you leave us, you abandon me, your family, I will have only one son. One son! That's not what a family— it isn't *fine*. It's terrible!

JESSICA: Yes. It is.

RACHEL: Josh. Please, oh Josh. My...my boy.

JOSH: No, it's...it's fine, I mean, it's not, no, but it's for the best. It's...it's just that...there's nothing. There's nothing. Everything else, the last few years, it's all kind of emptied out, somehow...the more I try to fill it, the quicker it empties out…and nothing's…nothing's left for me anymore. Here. I'm sorry, but you're not enough. Mom. None of you are enough; you can't be. I'm sorry, I've tried, I tried, you know, and nothing works anymore, nothing works here for me…I can't make it *mean* anything; *(He cries, embarrassed but unable to stop.)* How can you not *feel* it? How can any of you…I can't do it, I can't…I'm sorry, I'm sorry, I'm fine, I'm fine. I'm fine.

(JOSH squeezes his eyes in a vain attempt to stop the tears. RACHEL goes to comfort him. JESSICA stares ahead, unable to watch, resigned and placid.)

(Lights fade.)

Scene Three

(RACHEL's living room. BETH watching T V. After a moment, JOSH enters.)

JOSH: I heard the T V.

BETH: Too loud? Sorry.

JOSH: No, it's fine. *(Pause)* Where is, um, everyone?

BETH: *(Overlapping with "everyone")* In the kitchen.

JOSH: Everyone?

BETH: Yeah. Cleaning.

JOSH: Ethan too?

BETH: Yep.

JOSH: Then they're not cleaning. They're talking about me.

BETH: Oh, I don't know. After what hap—after dinner your mother focused on cleaning with what I can only describe as a Howard Hughes-like intensity.

JOSH: Well that I believe. When in doubt—and when it comes to emotions my mother's more or less always in doubt—feed it or clean it, that's her philosophy. You're not in helping?

BETH: Your mother insisted I "relax".

JOSH: So they can talk about me to Jessica. Poor Jessica. Anyway. *(Pause)*

BETH: You want to watch something?

JOSH: No. Well—news if you're not watching anything special.

BETH: No problem. *(She clicks the remote. Pause)*

JOSH: I don't know if this will surprise you based on what you've seen of me, but…I'm…I'm sorry about before.

BETH: Oh no, it's—

JOSH: Something about being here, this house, no, not at this house, anywhere, …I mean it must have been almost as tough to watch me as it was to be me.

BETH: No, it's—I owe you…I feel I owe you an apology.

JOSH: How so?

BETH: My ethnicity—not my ethnicity, but the way I sort of waved it like a red flag in your face before.

JOSH: No, it's—

BETH: It was calculated.

JOSH: Oh. What was it calculated to do, exactly?

BETH: I thought you were being a bit of a bully and I wanted to knock you down a peg. That's the only reason I said it—which isn't good enough. My connection to my roots, such as they are, is really as tenuous as…I mean, I like hummus, that's about the extent of it.

JOSH: Why…why aren't you more connected to your roots?

BETH: Oh…I don't know. Same reasons Ethan isn't, or Jessica, I guess.

JOSH: That's why I'm asking you.

BETH: Well, I'm afraid I don't have any insights for you. I keep in touch with a couple of people back where I grew up, in Michigan, although, not so much anymore, really. But, as far as…my ancestry, it would feel—I think to go overseas and claim some sort of allegiance with the people over there—people I've never met—would be…anyway, I can't see me doing it.

JOSH: You stopped yourself…what would it be?

BETH: Presumptuous. Smug. The, um, I don't know—I think there's enough shit going down in our lives, you know, state side, without poking our noses into their problems.

JOSH: But that's the thing—we are connected to them—that's the whole point. We pretend it's not our business—but nationality, or geography, that's just random and irrelevant, it's an artificial construct, it's—

BETH: "Artificial construct"? Wow, that's a conversational first for me, Josh, thanks— "artificial construct" —What pamphlet did that—and, I'm sorry—religion isn't an artificial construct?

JOSH: It's not just religion, and I don't think it is, no— it's a common history, a common—

BETH: I'm sorry. We shouldn't. This is stupid. Especially given what's gone on tonight. It's my fault, I apologize. These discussions never lead anywhere good, you know?

JOSH: O K.

BETH: I mean, you're not going to convince me, you know you're not going to convince me, and I certainly know I'm not going to convince you.

JOSH: O K. *(Pause)* And what would you be trying to convince me of?

BETH: I…I don't know, exactly.

JOSH: Precisely.

BETH: Well, O K then, even less point in carrying it on. I'm going to try to find Ethan and—

JOSH: Do you know Ethan never told any of us—didn't tell me, about your husband.

BETH: Well I didn't want him to.

JOSH: Why?

BETH: Because it's none of your business.

JOSH: Of course it is.

BETH: Well, now I'd love to hear how you've twisted it in your mind to have that make sense.

JOSH: Because—

BETH: Don't take this the wrong way, but who the fuck are you, Josh, to talk to me like that? Is the world some sort of big intervention to you now?

JOSH: I'm not—I don't feel like I have any sort of moral authority—I'm not trying to lead you anywhere.

BETH: I'm sorry but I don't quite believe that. And on top of it, it's useless. Saying you come across as a confrontational prick because deep down you're as scared and unsure as the rest of us doesn't help me too much. Because there's still the problem of you coming across as a confrontational prick.

JOSH: Why didn't you want us to know about Alec?

BETH: I refer you to my earlier comment.

JOSH: It's none of my business? You're wrong about that.

BETH: Am I?

JOSH: Yes.

BETH: How's that, exactly?

JOSH: I pushed people out of my way.

BETH: What's that mean?

JOSH: To get downstairs. After the elevators failed. I pushed past people. Not many, like three, I think, and not, you know, viciously, I didn't knock them down. But only because I didn't have to. They were slow and I didn't want to get caught behind them. One of them was this heavy set, older woman. Black. The other two were white men—not old men at all, thirties, forties maybe. They…were trying to help her. Help move her down the stairs. She was hurt, somehow, not too badly, but…she needed help. She was crying and praying. They asked me to—they needed me to help them. Just help them a little bit. I just…I shoved right past them. I don't know…it's a blur. These people. Who knows who they are, if they're alive. If they made it. Your husband, for all we'll ever know. I don't even—you'd think something like that—their faces would be burned in my mind, but for the life of me, I can't…it's a blur.

BETH: Christ. I…I wish I knew what I could say to that.

JOSH: Yeah.

(Pause)

BETH: You were just um, I mean it was just your instincts kicking in, you know. Survival. I'm sorry, I wish I knew…what to say.

JOSH: I've only told one other person about that day. Jessica. She said to me, she pulled me close to her and whispered "Baby as long as you're alive and safe".

I've since realized that was the moment I knew I could never love her again.

BETH: Yes. *(Pause)* You never... *(Pause)*

JOSH: What?

BETH: Why did you...you didn't say anything to anyone? At those um, support groups or?

JOSH: I don't—I stay away from those things. I can't, um...

BETH: Yeah. Me too.

JOSH: Yeah.

(Pause)

BETH: I'm sure that's a very healthy sign for both of us.

(JOSH *smiles.*)

JOSH: I'm sure.

(Lights fade)

Scene Four

(BETH *and* DR KIM *in* DR KIM's *office.*)

DR KIM: So. You saw Ethan when?

BETH: Few weeks ago. In January, late January—

DR KIM: Had you seen him since you broke things off?

BETH: Since we broke—yeah, no, I hadn't. We'd traded voicemails a little, but yeah. But he made me promise we'd go to the restaurant by his house in Jericho sometime, so. He'd just gotten back from moving his mother down to Florida and he had do a few things at the house before his sister-in-law, or ex-sister-in-law I guess she is, moved in, so we met up there at the restaurant. Which was pleasant enough, actually; he's a nice guy. Really good guy. We said we'd try to keep in touch.

DR KIM: But you don't see any potential there.

BETH: Nah. I think— I got the feeling he's with someone else now already.

(*As* DR KIM *responds to this, in muted conversation, the lights fade slightly as in the first scene and* BETH *turns to the audience:*)

BETH: This isn't working. I feel myself slip away from here; this used to be the one place—she used to be the one person—who I was honest with. Now I catch myself being polite. And now I sometimes hear her voice, not Alec's, which my guess is may be a good sign, but I can't bring myself to tell her, because whenever I hear her voice, it…

(*And now we hear* ALEC'*s voice from the opposite side of where* DR KIM *as he stands behind* BETH.)

ALEC: Tell her about Josh.

BETH: No…I don't know. Please. Oh Christ. I'm all alone. If you go away, I'll be all alone. How pathetic is that?

ALEC: You aren't alone. Tell Doctor Kim about Josh.

BETH: Josh?

ALEC: About his call.

BETH: That didn't mean any—it was nice of him but, frankly, weird and I…don't know what to…what to say about that. I'm not sure I even remember all of it.

ALEC: Beth.

BETH: It's true. It was early; I was half asleep, lying in bed.

(A cell phone rings. BETH *groggily picks it up. Looks at the number. She clearly doesn't recognize it. She tentatively answers it.)*

BETH: Hello?

(Now lights up on another part of the stage, revealing JOSH.*)*

JOSH: Hi, Beth?

BETH: Who is this, please?

JOSH: It's um, Josh.

BETH: Josh?

JOSH: Yeah, um, Josh Harkman. Ethan's brother. From Thanksgiving.

BETH: Oh, yeah, of course. Hey. What's um, what's going—where are you calling from?

JOSH: I'm, I'm sitting at a café. In Israel.

BETH: Jesus. Wow, Josh, that's a…that must be one kick ass phone plan you've got there.

JOSH: *(Small laugh)* Yeah. It's O K.

(Slight pause)

JOSH: I just wanted to— Sorry.	BETH: So, what's going— No, my bad, you go—

BETH: What's— is everything O K? Ethan's not here— we, um—

JOSH: No, I know, he told me.

BETH: Oh.

JOSH: It's…listen. I hope you don't mind me calling.

BETH: No it's, not at all.

JOSH: It's weird. My calling.

BETH: Well. It's just, um—

JOSH: It's not what you think.

BETH: Oh, um, O K. I'm not sure what I think. I'm a little groggy.

JOSH: Sorry. I've called too early.

BETH: No it's fine.

JOSH: I was just, this is going to sound strange, I know but um. It's just I was thinking about our conversation at Thanksgiving.

BETH: Oh God. Listen, Josh, whatever I said, I was just—

JOSH: I was thinking about how you, how you said you weren't connected to anything um, from your father's birthplace.

BETH: Oh. Yeah. Wow, That's kind of an unusual thing to remember.

JOSH: And I wanted to…I don't know. It struck me, what you said. Especially after I got here. And I wanted to…at the very least, I figured, now, you've um, gotten a phone call from here. From his birthplace, you know? You've been thought about in your ancestral home. Your, your voice has been heard there.

BETH: Oh, well…thanks. That was—that's thoughtful.

JOSH: No problem. *(Pause)* Well. So I figured if I called….you'd at least know.

BETH: Thank you.

JOSH: Well, I just wanted to do that.

BETH: No, thank you. That was very…sweet.

JOSH: I'm comfortable living with the fact that it's mostly weird.

BETH: Well, the two aren't mutually exclusive. And it's mostly sweet.

JOSH: That's not how Ethan saw it.

BETH: You told Ethan you were calling me?

JOSH: It's how I got the number.

BETH: Oh.

JOSH: Yeah, he thought of it more as:

(Lights on ETHAN, *also holding a phone. Though he's talking to* JOSH, *he is directly facing the audience.)*

ETHAN: Just another ten pounds of fucked up in the five pound bag of fucked up that is your life.

JOSH: Ethan.

ETHAN: What are you going to do? You gonna stalk my shiksa ex trans-Atlantically now?

BETH: He said that? I didn't think he was angry about us.

JOSH: I think it's more he's angry at me.

ALEC: What's it like there for him?

JOSH: That's not what this is, by the way.

BETH: *(To* ALEC*)* What?

JOSH: I said that's not what this is. I mean, stalking or—

BETH: Oh no, I don't think—

JOSH: Anything like that.

BETH: No. I know.

JOSH: Good. I just wanted you...to know. *(Pause)* Well, I should get going.

BETH: Of course.

JOSH: I mean, my cell plan's not that kick ass.

BETH: Yeah. Of course.

JOSH: We...I...

BETH: You sound, um. Good. You know, better.

JOSH: *(Although this is a bit of a barb, there's a good-natured quality to it that's been largely absent from our experiences with JOSH)* Better than the other time you spoke to me?

When I collapsed sobbing at my mother's dining room table? Not a very hard bar to clear.

ALEC: Talk to him.

JOSH: Well I um, I should—

ALEC: Beth.

BETH: Is it better for you? There?

JOSH: Better? Yes. In some ways. I don't, um. Not that it's perfect or...but yes.

BETH: Oh.

JOSH: I don't...it was never about what you thought it was about. Or Jessica, or Ethan or my mother or... anyone.

BETH: What did we think it was about?

JOSH: Escape, I think, maybe. I'm not sure. No one was really talking to me at the end.

BETH: Ethan mentioned your mother wasn't—she still not talking to you?

JOSH: Yes. Which she calls to remind me of a couple of times a month. She sent me a letter last week.

(RACHEL appears and recites her letter to JOSH directly to the audience)

RACHEL: I don't understand this Israel thing of yours— you need to grow up, my son. Your *father* wouldn't have understood, either. I understand how it must have traumatized you; of course it must have. It was horrible and unforgivable and shamelessly cruel. But you move on, don't you? You *have* to move on. Life's impossible otherwise. How the hell did people fight World War II? I mean, my God, Josh, how many

millions upon millions of people died in that? How
many people witnessed *tens* of thousands of horrible,
cruel, unspeakable deaths *every day* and *still* people
split the atom and wiped out the Nazis and came home
and invented the suburbs and started a baby boom?
And we're somehow supposed to wear black every
day and crawl to therapists or get divorced and leave
the *country* over three thousand people? Over *one* day?
What babies we are, if that's what's happened to us;
what weaklings. Your father and I failed you if this is
what you're reduced to. Love, Mom.

BETH: Well, she's hurt. Confused.

JOSH: Everyone is. It's inevitable. I've tried calling
Jessica but it went to voicemail. I sent here a long letter.
I finally got a text from her saying:

(JESSICA *appears and recites her text message to* JOSH
directly to the audience)

JESSICA: Please please please fuck fuck fuck fuck FUCK
you.

BETH: Wow. Like e.e.cummings with Turret's.

JOSH: Yeah. I tried calling her back, but the number's
been disconnected.

BETH: I'm sorry.

JOSH: Thanks.

BETH: And still…it—it's worth it to you.

JOSH: Yes. It's not that I— I can't honestly—I am…
lonely sometimes.

BETH: *(Suddenly, for no reason she's aware of, tears)* I'm
so…sorry to hear that.

JOSH: No, no it's O K. Really, it's O K. That's the whole
thing, Beth, that's the— here how I feel isn't the most
important thing. There's a community, there's no
striving for connection, there's only a war—a real

blood and bone war. There's something life affirming about living next to your enemies—you can't escape it by turning the channel or, or putting a flag pin on your lapel. I do feel lonely sometimes, but it's...I don't feel alone. I know that sounds a little...

BETH: No. It's...I think I understand.

JOSH: You said it was instinct at work when I pushed my way downstairs. But here...I feel I couldn't get away with it—not that there isn't cruelty and stupidity and cowardice here, too. Of course there is. But this is a tiny country pinned against the sea—you know? There's no room to shove your way past.

BETH: Maybe.

JOSH: Well, I should really go. I sent you an e-mail too, of some pictures I took of the landscape, I thought maybe you'd want to see where you come from.

BETH: Where I...thanks.

JOSH: Good luck to you, Beth. Shalom. (*And he is gone.*)

ALEC: Ah, that's it.

BETH: I guess so. Yes. (*Pause*) Shalom. (*Pause. To us:*) I knew what the word meant—or rather, I was vaguely aware of it—that it had multiple meanings.

ALEC: Hello and goodbye.

BETH: It kept bouncing around and around my head. So I google it. And I can't believe how many meanings it has:

ALEC: Hello.

BETH: Health.

ALEC: Completeness.

BETH: Harmony.

ALEC: Fullness.

BETH: Prosperity.

ALEC: Peace.

BETH: Farewell.

ALEC: Goodbye.

BETH: We don't have words like that in English—that can take in so many things. How can anything take in so much at once and not be whittled away? I don't even think such a thing is possible. Shalom. Peace, completeness. Hello.

ALEC: Goodbye.

BETH: The paradox of it: universal and intimate. The pride of endurance and the guilt of survival. White flakes snowing down from a warm blue sky.

ALEC: Goodbye.

(And now ALEC's *light fades completely.* BETH *stands alone in a single spotlight.)*

BETH: Sometimes, just as I start to fall asleep, I have a…vision of myself. A sort of waking dream because I know the whole time it's not real, and yet it feels true…I rise up from my bed over Manhattan, formless but…massive, somehow. And as I rise, I separate into uncountable particles of vapor. And yet I have density. And then the particles—my particles—are carried on cool startled gusts of wind everywhere: over New York, where I met Alec, over Jericho where Ethan and Josh grew up. West over rivers to Michigan and my parents, east across the ocean to Israel, everywhere, until finally I land, gentle and unfelt, on everyone… everyone I've ever loved—or tried to; everyone who's ever loved me, everyone I've ever forgiven; everyone from whom I've needed forgiveness. I reach them, I reach all of them, and I come to rest on their skin. None of them can feel me, but I do, I do come to rest. And my life…spreads out over them…like a benediction.

And then, only on those nights when that vision visits me, can I sleep peacefully. And in the instant before sleep, the last thought before I have no more thoughts, I think of Josh's call to me, and his e-mail. And some mornings, when I think I need it, I allow myself to read the last words again: Good luck to you. *Shalom.*

(Lights fade.)

END OF PLAY

www.ingramcontent.com/pod-product-compliance
Lightning Source LLC
Chambersburg PA
CBHW070024110426
42741CB00034B/2457